Bons Mots

A Contemporary Collection of Quotes

compiled by
Giles Dixon

Published by Wordzworth
www.wordzworth.com

Foreword

Most of the quotations in this book have been collected over the past twenty five years. They make up a small, but representative, sample of the quotes that I have posted on the website ContractStore.com during that period. The majority are from contemporary sources and were saved soon after they appeared in print, on the radio or elsewhere. Others are from earlier times which still have a relevance today.

My thanks are due to all those whose words and phrases appear in this collection and to those whose publications brought them to my attention, including, in particular, the Financial Times, The Guardian and the BBC.

I believe each of you has had something valuable to say, whether it be profound, troubling, witty, or simply worth repeating.

Giles Dixon.

Contents

Definitions

Artificial Intelligence

Artificial Intelligence is an oxymoron.

Available

"Available" means not Unavailable.

> *From a standard PPP contract*
> *prepared by a City law firm.*

Brain

The brain is an apparatus with which we think we think.

> *Ambrose Bierce, American writer*

Cliché

Clichés are where the truth goes to die.

> *David Runciman, How Democracy Ends*

1

Commission

A group of men that keep minutes and waste hours.

Committee

A committee is a cul-de-sac down which ideas are lured and then quietly strangled.

*Sir Barnett Cocks, from Order,
Order by Robert Rogers*

Confidence

Confidence is the prize given to the mediocre.

Robert Hughes, art critic

Confidence is what you have before you understand the problem.

Woody Allen

Dates

Dates are the pegs on which to hang your history.

Allan H. Long, school headmaster

Derivatives

Financial weapons of mass destruction.

Warren Buffet

Education

Education is what survives when what has been learned has been forgotten.

B.F.Skinner, American psychologist, FT 14.4.2011

Gentleman

A gentleman is someone who knows how to play the bagpipes but chooses not to.

Letter in FT

Humour

A weapon of mass distraction.

Pieter-Dirk Uys

Jury

12 persons summoned at random to decide which party has the better lawyer.

Hilaire Belloc, poet

Lawyer

A lawyer is like a rhinoceros – short-sighted, thick-skinned, and ever ready to charge.

Sir Malcolm Rifkind

Legend

Legends are there to tell us what history has forgotten.

Elif Shafak, The Island of Missing Trees

Monarchy

The monarchy is the light above politics.

Roger Scruton

Non-executive Directors

They are like bidets – no one knows what they're for, but they add a touch of class.

Martin Lukes (aka Lucy Kellaway), FT 16.7.2007

Peace

Peace is merely the interval while everyone is reloading.

Letter in FT

Pop Art

Nostalgia for now.

Pauline Boty, artist

Quantitative Easing

Quantitative Easing is like filling a car with petrol when the tank has been disconnected from the engine.

Simon Jenkins, The Guardian

Science

Science is the poetry of reality.

Richard Dawkins

Social Media

A window for narcissism

Matthieu Ricard, Lunch with the FT 5.6.2020

Stockbroker

Someone who invests your money until it is all gone.

Woody Allen

Venture Capital

The final redoubt of individuals with discipline and ambition but no actual talent.

Antonio Garcia Martinez, 'Chaos Monkeys: Inside the Silicon Valley Money Machine'.

Weed

A weed is a flower in the wrong place.

George Washington Carver, American scientist

Arts

I don't believe in genius. I believe in freedom. I think anyone can do it – anyone can be like Rembrandt.

Damien Hirst, interview in The Guardian

I know little about art, and I don't even know what I like.

Simon Hoggart, The Guardian

Never under-estimate the power of a large gold frame.

Banksy — from one of his works (in a large gold frame) on show at the Bristol Museum

Flesh is the reason oil paint was invented.

Willem de Kooning, Dutch-American Artist

Stay ahead of the avant garde.

The personal motto of the artist Peter Blake

When your painting first sells for over a million, that's when they start calling you Mr. Tuymans.

Luc Tuymans, Belgian Artist,
Lunch with the FT 11.2.2011

You'll never have a good art career unless your work fits into the elevator of a New York apartment block.

Grayson Perry, artist, Reith lectures

ARTS

He [Jeff Koons] shows what happens when
money and celebrity become yardsticks for
culture. It is not a pretty sight.

Jackie Wullsschlagger, FT 28.11.2014

The English don't understand music,
but they love the noise it makes.

Sir Thomas Beecham, composer

He roamed while his fiddle burned.

*This was said of a musician
(Vaughan Williams?) who was known
to have had a number of affairs.*

All art is modern art at some point.

Steven Wright, US Comedian

Music makes people less obsessed with
consumerism because a performance is
not a consumable or ownable. It's not a
commodity.

Ian Bostridge,
Lunch with the FT 8.11.2013

Those who watch television lose the world,
those who read gain it.

Werner Herzog Interview, FT 16.3.2007

Too much of reality television puts inflated
egos in empty spaces and pumps them
up further to see who explodes first.

John Lloyd, FT 28.11.2009

If it weren't for electricity, we'd all be
watching television by candlelight.

George Gobel, American Humorist

Less is more.

Ludwig Mies van der Rohe,
German-American Architect

The difference between good and bad
architecture is the time you spend on it.

David Chipperfield, Architect

I would say that part of the very definition
of "good design" is that it produces
value, and that design that celebrates
little apart from itself is bad design.

Paul Morrell, Chief Construction
Adviser to the UK Government

Books & Writing

The art of writing is the art of applying the seat of one's trousers to the seat of one's chair.

Kingsley Amis, writer

For me, a book is a room in your head that holds secrets.

John Lanchester, interview in FT 29.8.2014

To be a good writer you first have to love words, then you'll find you have something to say. If you start out with something to say you end up with journalism or propaganda.

Peter Porter, Australian poet

Everybody does have a book in them, but in most cases that's where it should stay.

Christopher Hitchens, writer

When I want to read a novel, I write one.

Benjamin Disraeli

Immature poets imitate. Mature poets steal.

T.S. Eliot

To steal ideas from one person is plagiarism; to steal from many is research.

Robert Hughes,
attributed to Wilson Mizner,
American playwright

Great writers are the saints for the godless.

Anita Brookner, writer

How very stupid of me not to have thought of that myself.

Thomas Huxley,
on reading Charles Darwin's Origin of Species

Language

Latin has no place in the teaching of modern English, per se.

Martin Clunes on BBC Radio 4
Have I Got News for You

Nowadays it seems that almost any noun can be verbed.

Anon

To name things wrongly is to add to the misfortune of the world.

Albert Camus

The great enemy of clear language is insincerity. When there is a gap between one's real and one's declared aims, one turns, as it were, instinctively to long words and exhausted idioms, like a cuttlefish squirting out ink.

George Orwell

Language is the skin on my thought.

Arundhati Roy, The Algebra of Infinite Justice

Business & Work

The customer is always right.

H.G.Selfridge, the founder of Selfridges store in London

The customer's usually wrong.

Michael O'Leary, chief of Ryanair

Stores are never nice to people,
they are nice to credit cards.

Richard Gere in Pretty Woman

We have a very Darwinian menu.
Whatever sells, we put on the menu;
whatever doesn't sell, we take off.

Chris Kempczinski, CEO of McDonalds,
Lunch with the FT 27.11.2020

Technology companies begin to die
when salespeople and bean counters
start making the decisions.

Steve Jobs, founder of Apple

Formula for success:
Rise early, work hard, strike oil.

John Paul Getty, oil magnate

The way to make a small fortune in
publishing is to start with a large one.

Anthony Blond, publisher

Don't look for a needle in a haystack.
Buy the haystack.

John Bogle, founder,
Vanguard Group, FT 4.5. 2024

You don't create a tiger by inflating a cat.

Nick Jarrett-Kerr, from a talk
on law firm mergers

The brain is a wonderful organ. It starts
working the moment you get up in the
morning and does not stop until you get
into the office.

Robert Frost, American poet

I am not interested in having a career....
I think a career is something your father
brings home in a briefcase every night,
looking kind of tired.

Sean Parker, founder of Napster,
Lunch with the FT 4.3.2011

If you want to grow your business,
remember that 1 plus 1 is 11, not 2.

A Chinese entrepreneur

Be careful how you treat those on the way
up as you might meet them on the way
down.

Anon

Work for something because it is good,
not just because it stands a chance to
succeed.

Vaclav Havel, former president
of the Czech Republic

If you get arrogant, you lose your
way and start making mistakes.

Richard Fuld, CEO of Lehman Brothers,
interviewed in Euromoney

You can't produce a baby in one month by getting nine women pregnant.

Warren Buffett, American business magnate

This is worse than a divorce. I've lost half my net worth and I still have a wife.

From a trader on a BBC website

A criminal is a person with predatory instincts; but without sufficient capital to form a corporation.

Clarence Seward Darrow, American lawyer

A sane man doesn't give his money to the poor – a sane man takes money from the poor.

W. Somerset Maugham, from his play, Sheppey

I have nothing to complain about when I get home from a hard day's work, because I do not work hard, and I am already home.

Tim Dowling, Guardian Weekend

Economics

The only function of economic forecasting is to make astrology look respectable.

John Kenneth Galbraith

Economics, essentially a faith-based discipline, represented itself as a hard science.

Philip Stephens, FT 18.2.2021

When you find anyone agreeing with you, change your mind.

John Maynard Keynes

There's no point in being an economist if you can't manipulate statistics.

Merryn Somerset Webb, FT 28.6.2013

We are mired in a malaise, from which we are not likely to emerge any time soon.

Joseph Stiglitz, in a review of Martin Wolf's book, The Shifts & The Shocks, FT 29.8.2014

Why did nobody notice?

H.M. Queen Elizabeth's question on the 2008 financial crash to the director of research at the London School of Economics

Limitless growth is the fantasy of economists, businesses and politicians.

Vandana Shiva, philosopher, The Guardian

I agree that they [economic forecasts] are not worth the paper they are written on.

Lord Mervyn King, former governor of the Bank of England, BBC World Service November 2023

Almost everyone in Sweden has more than the average number of legs.

Prof. Hans Rosling in a talk on statistics

Environment

I'm truly sorry man's dominion,
Has broken Nature's social union.

Robert Burns, in a poem to a mouse

People who live by a riverside have always
two pleasures to command: they can look
both upstream and down.

Freya Stark, from Baghdad Sketches 1937

The best time to plant a tree is twenty
years ago. The second best time is now.

*African proverb – quoted by
Dambisa Moyo in her book 'Dead Aid'*

The best thing about the Earth is if you poke holes in it oil and gas comes out.

Steve Stockman, American politician

The 'control of nature' is a phrase conceived in arrogance, born of the Neanderthal age of biology and philosophy, when it was supposed that nature exists for the convenience of man.

Rachel Carson,
from Silent Spring, first published 1962.

We are the only species of living creatures that even conceives of exerting control over the environment thrust upon it. Admittedly this control is far from complete. Its extension is greatly to be desired.

Thomas Midgley Jr., inventor of leaded petrol
in 1921 and of CFCs in 1928 (from Prometheans
in the Lab by Sharon Bertsch McGrayne)

Our backs have to be against the wall
before we can read the writing on it.

*Helen Zille, prime minister, Western Cape, BBC
Newsnight, discussing the Cape Town drought*

We may be the first species to document
our own extinction.

Lily Cole, from her book Who Dares Wins

The greater the number of species that
become extinct, the closer we become to
extinction.

Gerald Durrell, writer

The biggest handicap that conservation
faces is that we humans still consider
ourselves to be separate from the rest of
life, and the rest of life is merely there to
support us. It is infantile arrogance.

Chris Packham, Guardian interview

There is no exception to the rule that every organic being naturally increases at so high a rate, that if not destroyed, the earth would soon be covered by the progeny of a single pair.

Even slow-breeding man has doubled in 25 years, and at this rate, in a few thousand years, there would literally not be standing room for his progeny.

Charles Darwin, On the Origin of the Species, published 1859

It is slowly dawning on us that the human population is growing, and our need to burn things in order to survive is going to outweigh the ability of new things to grow.

Antony Gormley, Interview, FT 4.5.2007

We will become independent of nature

The Cyprus Minister of Agriculture, when discussing his Government's plans to deal with the island's severe water shortage.

If you sweep Mother Nature out of the door with a broom, she will come back through the window with a pitchfork.

Old Russian proverb

Once the rhetoric has settled and the delegates have drifted away,
the indignation cools and the world carries on business as usual.

Mohamed Nasheed, President of the Maldives, speaking at a climate change summit in September 2009.

You'll never find an insurer saying,
'I don't believe in climate change.'

John Neale, CEO Lloyds of London FT 14.6.2024

There is no business on a dead planet.

Petter Stordalen, BBC Radio 4, Desert Island Discs

Doing nothing is not an option.

> *Maathai Wangari, Kenyan activist*
> *who won the Nobel Peace Prize*

We are already on the last bus, but if
we all got together and acted now and
governments followed, then we still
have a chance.

> *Randal Plunkett, Baron of Dunsany,*
> *interviewed on his rewilding of 750*
> *acres at Dunsany, Irish Times*

Finance & Money

There's an old saying that Wall Street
wants to combine its experience with the
clients' money and turn that into Wall
Street's money and the clients'
experience. And I think that's wrong.

Bill Priest, interview in FT 15.2.2018

I used to think I would like to be rich, but
now that I've met some rich people I'm not
so sure about that.

*Mma Makuti in The Kalahari Typing School
for Men by Alexander McCall Smith*

All I ask is the chance to prove that money can't make me happy.

Spike Milligan

Debt is like a crazy aunt we keep down in the basement. All the neighbours know she's there, but nobody wants to talk about her.

Ross Perot, American business magnate, with thanks to Jeff Randall, Daily Telegraph

High finance is just a game of noughts and crosses. The market adds a lot of noughts to your fortune, then it comes back and crosses them off!

Sir James Goldsmith, French-British tycoon

Money doesn't grow on trees – unless you are an olive farmer.

Cypriot proverb

Bankers are exceptionally greedy with over-inflated opinions of their talents pegged to an exaggerated sense of their importance in the economic scheme of things.

Will Hutton, from Them and Us: Changing Britain – Why We Need a Fair Society

The main problem with banks is incompetence: in the good times they lend money to people who can't afford to repay it. Now they refuse to lend to those who can.

Anon

The difference between tax avoidance and tax evasion is the thickness of a prison wall.

Denis Healey, former Chancellor of the Exchequer

After you have about $5m to $10m, your lifestyle doesn't really change that much.

Clive Palmer, Australian minerals magnate and politician, FT 28.6.2014

Millionaires are often millionaires because they had no other option.

Theo Paphitis, British retail magnate and entrepreneur

I know well many of the mega-rich and, by and large, they are very decent people. Most wouldn't mind being told to pay more in taxes, particularly when so many of their fellow citizens are truly suffering.

Warren Buffett, American business magnate

Gardens

At Kew on the right bank of the river, man created a garden of Eden, at Brentford on the left, he created a Hell.

Cecil Roberts, The Road to Bath

No garden, however small, should contain less than two acres of rough woodland.

The first Lord Rothschild

It is very fascistic. You take out the weak and the strong remain. It's like ethnic cleansing.

Lars von Trier, film director, on vegetable gardening

When I started gardening I knew everything there was to know about very little; as I grew older I found I knew less and less about more and more, and now I know nothing about everything.

Alwyn, Allotments-UK forum

It is not the business of the botanist to eradicate the weeds.

C. Northcote Parkinson

The best fertiliser is the shadow of the gardener.

Chinese proverb

The difference between a good garden and a bad one is a fortnight.

attributed to Bob Flowerdew on Gardener's Question Time, BBC Radio 4

Law

A retreat from the rule of law, human rights and civil liberties is short-sighted and unthinkable. Yet such a retreat is precisely what is taking place. A quiet and relentless war is being waged on our rights.

Baroness Helena Kennedy KC,
from her book Just Law

The making of laws is like the making of sausages—the less you know about the process the more you respect the result.

Attributed to Otto von Bismark, first
Chancellor of the German Empire

From shopping in a store to running a corporation, contracts and agreements matter everywhere.

Oliver Hart, 2016 Nobel Prize winner for Economics

A verbal contract is not worth the paper it is written on.

Samuel Goldwyn, American film producer

If a law is of such a nature that it requires you to be the agent of injustice to another, then I say, break the law.

Henry David Thoreau, American naturalist & philosopher

It's just 99% of lawyers who give the rest a bad name.

Clive Anderson, from Simon Hoggart, The Guardian

The art of cross-examination is not to examine crossly.

Sir John Mortimer QC

In the English system you're innocent until proved Irish.

Michael Mansfield KC

Judgments of the Supreme Court are not final because they are right; they are right because they are final.

Joshua Rozenberg, Law Society Gazette

Judge to accused: "Do you plead guilty or not guilty?"

Accused replies: "I couldn't say, your Honour. I haven't heard the evidence yet."

Patrick Hughes, from his book
More on Oxymoron

Human rights law tends to be applied
to rather unattractive and unpleasant
people.

Lord (Ken) Clarke , former
Chancellor of the Exchequer

At his best, man is the noblest of all
animals; separated from law and justice
he is the worst.

Aristotle

It was so cold in Ottawa last winter that
I even saw a lawyer with his hands in his
own pockets.

With thanks to Ray Pearmain,
resident of Ottawa

The law is human and flawed. Just like
newspapers or medicine or the internet,
it embodies all that is brilliant and awful
about humankind.

Ian McEwan, writer

Living & Dying

Youth is a wonderful thing. What a crime to waste it on children.

George Bernard Shaw

Birthdays are good for you – the more you have, the longer you live.

Anon

If you resolve to give up smoking, drinking and loving, you don't actually live longer; it just seems like it.

Clement Freud, British broadcaster and writer

My expectations were reduced to zero
when I was 21. Everything since then has
been a bonus.

Stephen Hawking, theoretical physicist

You are never going to be younger or
healthier than you are now.

*Michael Martin, investment
manager, FT 15.8.2019*

More people would live to a ripe old age if
they weren't too busy providing for it.

Anon

Is life worth living? It depends upon the
liver.

Anon

Even I don't look like Cindy Crawford in the morning

Cindy Crawford

My life has been one long descent into respectability.

Mandy Rice-Davies, Welsh model

Wrinkles are hereditary: parents get them from their children.

Doris Day

The first half of our lives are ruined by our parents and the second half by our children.

Clarence Seward Darrow, American lawyer

It is sad to grow old but nice to ripen.

Brigitte Bardot, French film star

70 may be the new 60, but 80 is still
eighty

Giles Dixon

Age is a high price to pay for maturity.

Tom Stoppard, playwright

I attribute my long and continuing life to
my prudent avoidance of cricket and all
other forms of sport.

Barry Humphries

I've never seen so many dead people
smoking.

*Ronnie Scott, jazz musician to his
expatriate audience in Abu Dhabi*

I never wanted to be old, but I couldn't stop it.

Edna O'Brien, Lunch with the FT 14.7.2017

Life is too short to stuff a mushroom.

Shirley Conran, writer

I always thought old age would take longer

Anon- from Mexico thanks to Barry Humphries.

Your time is limited, so don't waste it living someone else's life.

Steve Jobs, founder of Apple

Death is nature's way of telling you to slow down.

Anon, from 'More on Oxymoron'
by Patrick Hughes

At my age I do what Mark Twain did: I get my daily paper, look at the obituaries page and if I'm not there I carry on as usual.

Sir Patrick Moore, British
astronomer and writer

Overheard after a moving
service at a crematorium:

"That was a funeral to die for."

Die, my dear doctor?
That is the last thing I shall do.

Lord Palmerston

Always be sure to go to other people's
funerals, otherwise they won't come to yours.

Yogi Berra, American baseball player

Overheard at a funeral:

"Are you a friend of the corpse?"

Memorial services are the cocktail parties
of the geriatric set.

Sir Harold MacMillan

As my mother likes to say, eternity is
awfully long, especially near the end.

Matthieu Ricard, Lunch with FT 5.6.2020

Married woman, overheard at a party:

"When one of us dies, I'm going to
live in the south of France."

When told by his host that it was a great honour
to have accepted his invitation to lunch on
his 90th birthday, Sir John Gielgud replied:

"Oh, I'm delighted to have been asked. All
my real friends are dead, you know."

Gyles Brandreth, English
broadcaster (who was the host)

The cemeteries are full of
indispensable men.

Pier Ferdinando Casini, Italian politician

Love & Marriage

Marriage isn't a thing to be romantic about – it lasts too long.

John Hankin, from his play
The Charity that Began at Home

Chains do not hold a marriage together. It is threads, hundreds of tiny threads, which sew people together through the years.

Simone Signoret, French actress

A widow in search of a new man should look for one who has a full head of hair – and a full bank account.

Anon

'I'm going to get married,' he heard himself say, and the doors to his future clanged shut in his face.

Anita Brookner, Incidents in the Rue Laugier

When a man opens a car door for his wife, it's either a new car or a new wife.

HRH Prince Philip

He who has a yacht has a different wife every night.

Modern Greek proverb, Taki, The Spectator

When your wife is quiet, don't interrupt.

Paul Bailey, writer, on BBC Radio 4

A husband is not like a tablecloth. You
don't want to change him every fortnight.

*Shazia Mirza's mother, with acknowledgements
to Shazia Mirza and The Guardian*

Q: What is the penalty for bigamy?
A: Two wives.

Anon (French)

A divorce is like an amputation,
you survive but there is less of you.

Margaret Atwood, writer, from Surfacing

Overheard: "Did you sleep with him?"
"Not a wink."

From a letter in The Guardian

If all the girls who attended the Yale prom were laid end to end, I wouldn't be at all surprised.

Dorothy Parker, American writer

Opportunity only gives you knockers once.

Pamela Anderson, actress, when asked what is the most important lesson life has taught her. The Guardian

There are two things people always pay for, food and sex. I wasn't any good at cooking.

Madame Claude, a celebrated 20th century Paris brothel keeper

Good girls go to Heaven.
Bad girls go everywhere.

Helen Gurley Brown, author of Sex & the Single Girl

What does the Canadian girl say when you ask her if she'd like sex? "Only if you're having some yourself."

Margaret Atwood in The Guardian

Philosophy

There is no liberty without morality, and no freedom without responsibility.

Rabbi Lord Jonathan Sacks, BBC Radio 4

Questions you cannot answer are usually far better for you than answers you cannot question.

Yuval Noah Harari,
21 Lessons for the 21st Century

I've been able to have a very relaxed philosophy, which is to enjoy yourself as much as you can without damaging other people.

Diana Athill, writer, at 100, Guardian interview

I spent a big chunk of my life studying philosophy and I'm still recovering.

Robert Armstrong, FT 6.11.2020

It is one of the pervasive features of philosophy that nothing in it is ever entirely satisfactory.

Jim Hankinson, Bluff your way in Philosophy

When I play with my cat, who knows whether she is not amusing herself with me more than I with her.

Michel de Montaigne, French philosopher

If a man begin with certainties, he shall end in doubts; but if he will be content to begin with doubts, he shall end in certainties.

Francis Bacon, The Advancement of Learning.

I have a new philosophy. I'm only going to dread one day at a time.

Charles M. Schulz, American cartoonist

To experience sublime natural beauty is to confront the total inadequacy of language to describe what you see.

Eleanor Catton, writer & Man Booker prize winner, article in The Guardian

The future is the only certain thing that does not exist.

Otto Dov Kulka, Israeli historian

I esteem the observations of great men more than I do their conclusions. Minds possessed of genius observe with exactitude and assurance; indeed when they outline the pros and cons of a matter for us, we are able to draw conclusions for ourselves.

C.P.Cavafy, Greek poet

Think you are too small to make a
difference? Try sleeping with a mosquito.

The Dalai Lama

Politics

United Kingdom

We have a democracy but it's dysfunctional. The structure is such that the pressure is on the MP to conform with the Party, rather than hold Government to account on behalf of his constituents.

Lord (Zac) Goldsmith (when he was an MP).

The English nation thinks it is free, but it is greatly mistaken, for it is only during the election of members of parliament; as soon as they are elected it is enslaved and counts for nothing.

Jean-Jaques Rousseau, The Social Contract

The main essentials of a prime minister
are sleep and a sense of history.

Harold Wilson, from Order!
Order! by Robert Rogers

As ever, power is exercised by those who
want power. And anyone who wants power
definitely ought to be denied it.

Jeremy Paxman,
FT 13.2.2015

There is now a well-ingrained popular
view across the country that our political
institutions and their politicians are
failing, untrustworthy, and disconnected
from the great mass of the British people.

From the Introduction of Power to
the People, an Independent Inquiry
into Britain's Democracy, 2006

I now want more time to devote
to politics and more freedom to do so.

*Tony Benn in 1999 on his
retirement as an MP after 47 years*

The problem with socialism is that
eventually you run out of other
people's money.

Margaret Thatcher

He believes his future as a
politician is behind him.

*Comment by Sir John Major's spokesperson on
the suggestion he might run as mayor of London*

One of the dark lessons of (political)
leadership is that in their beginnings lie
the seeds of their end.

Steve Richards, The Guardian

Political language is designed to make lies sound truthful and murder respectable, and give an appearance of solidity to pure wind.

George Orwell

We should silence anyone who opposes the right to freedom of speech.

Sir Boyle Roche,
Irish politician who died in 1807

The country is going down the drain and they are squabbling about the size of the plughole.

Jeremy Thorpe, former Leader
of the Liberal Party

All political careers end in failure.

Enoch Powell, former MP

On Sir Winston Churchill

The mediocrity of his thinking is concealed
by the majesty of his language.

*Aneurin Bevan on a speech
by Churchill, with thanks
to Robert Rogers*

Churchill never doubted his own genius,
though subordinates sometimes wished
he would.

*`Max Hastings 'Finest Years:
Churchill as Warlord 1940-45'*

It would be a great reform in politics if
wisdom could be made to spread as easily
and as rapidly as folly.

Sir Winston Churchill

International

For more than two centuries, the US
and Europe have exercised an effortless
economic, political and cultural hegemony.
That era is coming to an end.

Philip Stephens, FT 9.10.2008

Planet Earth is big enough for two
countries to succeed, and one country's
success is an opportunity for the other.

*Xi Jinping, President of China at a meeting
in California with US President Joe Biden*

The trouble with free election is that you
never know who is going to win.

*Leonid Brezhnev, Soviet politician and former
Secretary-General of the Communist Party*

Power is a great aphrodisiac

Henry Kissinger, former US Secretary of State

We must avoid arrogance.
Vanity leads to mistakes.

> *Sheikh Tamim bin Hamad al-Thani, Emir*
> *of Qatar (in an inaugural speech after*
> *his father abdicated in his favour)*

Ignorance allied with power
is the most ferocious enemy of justice.

> *James Baldwin, American writer*

Whoever you vote for,
the government always gets in.

> *Anon*

You campaign in poetry.
You govern in prose.

> *Mario Cuomo, American lawyer and*
> *former Governor of New York*

What's troubling is the gap between the

magnitude of our problems

and the smallness of our politics.

Barack Obama,
from his book The Audacity of Hope

The Constitution does not just protect

those whose views we share;

it also protects those with

whose views we disagree.

Edward Kennedy, American Senator

La démocratie est le système

le plus bottom up de la terre.

Emmanuel Macron, President of France

Democracy is like a bus, we will get off
when we get to our destination.

Recep Tayyip Erdogan, President of Turkey

We fought for freedom and all we got was
democracy.

*Comment from the floor at an election rally
in South Africa (Pieter-Dirk Uys, FT)*

We know what to do, we just don't know
how to get re-elected once we have done it.

*Jean-Claude Juncker,
when prime minister of Luxembourg*

To win an election you need addition
and multiplication, to lose you need
subtraction and division.

*Comment on the
US presidential election, BBC Radio 4*

If I know the answer, I'll answer you,
if I don't I'll just respond.

> **Donald Rumsfeld, American
> politician on the BBC**

Christmas is when kids tell Santa what
they want and adults pay for it. Deficits
are when governments tell adults what
they want, and their kids pay for it.

> **Richard Lamm, American politician**

Never let a good crisis go to waste.

> **Rahm Emmanuel, President
> Obama's Chief of Staff**

I'm from the government and
I'm here to help.

> **The most terrifying words in the English
> language, according to Ronald Reagan**

Less inequality is likely to make economies work better by increasing the ability of the entire population to participate, on more equal terms. An important condition for this, in turn, is that politics not be unduly beholden to wealth.

Martin Wolf FT 25.4.2014

Religion

All religions are a pathway
to arrive at God.

Pope Francis

The duty of a Christian is not
to succeed, but to fail cheerfully.

Robert Louis Stevenson

Prejudice, a dirty word, and faith, a clean
one, have something in common:
they both begin where reason ends.

Harper Lee, Go Set a Watchman

When a thousand people believe some made-up story for a month – that's fake news. When a billion people believe it for a thousand years – that's a religion.

Yuval Noah Harari, 21 Lessons for the 21st Century

Physics is not a religion, If it were, we would have a much easier time raising money.

Leon Lederman, physicist BBC Radio 4

Religion is the frozen thought of man out of which they build temples.

Jiddu Krishnamurti, Indian philosopher

How do you make God laugh? Tell him your plans for the future.

Ken Dodd, comedian, on BBC Radio 4

Better a genius without faith than a
believer without talent.

*Father Alain Couturier, the Dominican
monk, commenting on the selection of
artists and architects for French church
buildings in an article in Harpers Bazaar*

When the white missionaries came to
Africa, they had the Bible and we had the
land. They said, 'Let us pray.' We closed
our eyes. When we opened them, we had
the Bible and they had the land.

Bishop Desmond Tutu

If a God has made this world, then I would
not like to be the God; its misery and
distress would break my heart.

Arthur Schopenhauer

If you don't marry me I'll become a priest.

*Jorge Mario Bergoglio (later Pope
Francis) in a letter to Amalia Damonte
when they were both 12 years old.*

Just for the record,
I'm not in favour of sin.

Justin Welby, Archbishop of
Canterbury, BBC Radio 4

Travel

Q:"Did you have a good holiday?" A: "Well, there's no point in having a bad one, is there."

Overheard on a ship-to-shore radio, Doubtful Sound, New Zealand

Tourism is sin, walking is virtue.

Werner Herzog, German film director quoted by Bruce Chatwin, English travel writer

I would feel rather more rested after a two-week break if I didn't have to take myself on holiday with me.

John Crace, The Guardian

As I sat, strapped in my seat waiting during the countdown, one thought kept crossing my mind ... every part of this rocket was supplied by the lowest bidder.

John Glenn, the first American to orbit the Earth

Asked by a young couple on a country lane in Essex how long it would take to get to the next village, a local man working in a field paused and then replied:

"If you walks for 'alf an hour and sits down for 'alf an hour, it'll take longer."

Passengers are reminded that they are here to wait for the train. The train is not here to wait for them.

A London Underground train driver.

Heathrow is the noisiest airport in Europe because of the number of people living under its flight paths.

Report in FT 22.4.2013

When you have time to go fishing, you don't have the money. And when you have the money, you don't have the time.

Jeremy Paxman, broadcaster

I like working on holiday because it makes me feel important.

Tim Dowling, The Guardian

Blackpool is what America would be like if it were poor.

Simon Hoggart, The Guardian

War

It will be a war in which we risk almost everything of which we are proud, and in which we stand to gain nothing.

Manchester Guardian leading article 5 August 1914

War is organised murder, and nothing else.

Harry Patch, the last surviving soldier from of the First World War, who died at the age of 111 on 25 July 2009

God and Country are an unbeatable team; they break all records for oppression and bloodshed.

Luis Bunuel, Spanish film director

War is God's way of teaching the
Americans geography.

Heard on BBC Radio 4

The failure of the US's foreign adventures
often seems to have its roots in their total
ignorance of things on the ground, of the
countries they fiddle with.

Peter Carey, Australian writer,
Guardian interview

A Palestinian and an Israeli asked God
whether there would ever be peace between
them. He replied "Of course, but not in my
lifetime."

With thanks to Simon Schama

Crime against humanity
is a bourgeois notion.

One of the Farc Guards who held
Ingrid Betancourt captive in the
Colombian jungle for six years

I tell you what, you do the fighting
and I'll do the talking.

*Prime Minister David Cameron at
a meeting with defence chiefs*

Kill one man and you're a murderer,
kill a million and you're a conqueror.

Jean Rostand, French biologist

In victory, you deserve champagne,
in defeat you need it.

Napoleon Bonaparte

Dialogue is the strategy of the brave.

Jonas Gahr Store, Norwegian Foreign Minister

Odds & Ends

People who think they know everything are profoundly annoying to those of us who actually do.

An unnamed barrister, Law Society Gazette

Overheard:

Mother to 4 year old daughter: "Why are you crying?"

Daughter: "I'm a child and I am meant to cry."

Not to find joy in difference is a surrender to ignorance.

Howard Jacobson, BBC Radio 4

I always respect other people's opinions,
even when I think they are talking bollocks.

Mick Channon, horse race trainer
– from his biography

Jean Paul Sartre to waitress in cafe:
"Coffee with no cream, please."

Waitress: "We have no cream today,
monsieur".

Sartre: "How about coffee with no milk?"

from More on Oxymoron, by Patrick Hughes

People have one thing in common:
they are all different.

Robert Zend, Canadian poet

Never give more than one excuse.

Sarah Hegarty

Today is better than tomorrow.

*A participant in the documentary film
"Iraq in Fragments" by James Longley*

What matters is not how well you are
playing when you are playing well,
but how well you are playing when you
are playing badly.

*Martina Navratilova, tennis player,
as quoted by Clive James on BBC Radio 4*

Muhammad Ali walks into a restaurant
for a cup of coffee.

Waitress: "We don't serve black people"

Muhammad Ali: "And I don't eat them!"

*As told by Muhammad Ali, boxer,
on Michael Parkinson TV show.*

Bear in mind the gambler's advice:
If you don't know who is the patsy
in the room, it's you.

John Kay, FT 30.7.2007

In the old days we was nice to the nice people and we was nasty to the nasty people. Nowadays we have to be nice to everyone.

A recently retired policeman, with thanks to Theodore Dalrymple, The Spectator

Human Relations are difficult -and some of our relations are not even human.

Anon

She is the most balanced person I know – she has a chip on both shoulders.

With thanks to Adele Buckell

Take a bottle of Napoleon Brandy, pour into a silver salver, swill and throw away.

The opening words of a recipe for trifle attributed to Mrs Beeton

There are three sides to every argument:
my side, your side and the truth.

Anon

It was far better than being psycho-
analysed. It gave me a completely
new idea of myself.

Edith Evans, on posing nude for a
sculpture by Dora Gordine in 1938

A patient asked their surgeon:

"How often do patients die
during an operation?"

The Surgeon replied: "Just once."

In theory there is no difference between
theory and practice. In practice there is.

Attributed to Yogi Berra

Does anyone ever know what he needs
to know until he has the opportunity
to know it?

Brian Sewell on art in the Evening Standard

There are two ways of doing everything,
and the wrong one usually comes first.

George Dixon

Ask not what you can do for your country.
Ask what is for lunch

Orson Welles

If I want your opinion, I'll give it to you.

Attributed to Sam Goldwyn

A super intelligent machine could be the
last invention humans ever make.

Martin Rees in his book, Our Final Century

You have to decide even to hesitate.

Stanislaw Lec, Polish writer,
from More on Oxymoron by Patrick Hughes

Man is the only animal that blushes.
Or needs to.

Mark Twain

I am called Spiderman, not because I
am lithe and active, but because I find it
difficult to get out of the bath.

Gary Richardson, BBC Radio 4

The first time I see a jogger smiling,
I'll try it.

Joan Rivers

I like to run just often enough to make me feel smug.

Jack Dee, on the News Quiz,
BBC Radio 4

Nothing would be done at all if one waited until one could do it so well that no one could find fault with it.

John Henry Newman

The main thing is to keep the main thing the main thing.

Stephen Covey,
The 7 Habits of Highly Effective People

Swearing is a weakness – a sign that the brain isn't working fast enough to construct a decent sentence and get your point across.

The Secret Footballer, The Guardian

My month without alcohol went so well
that I finished early.

Tim Dowling, The Guardian

Twitter is not just a phoney form of
conversation, it is a deceptive
medium for discussion.

Harry Eyres, FT 8.7.2011

I burned the candle at both ends and it
often gave a lovely light.

Christopher Hitchens

If you don't have anything nice to say,
let's hear it.

Peter Brookes, on BBC Radio 4

I'd rather cry in a Rolls than be happy on
a bicycle.

*Patrizia Reggiani, widow of
Gucci heir Maurizio Gucci*

You can always tell a Yorkshireman – but
you can't tell him much!

Anon

She was fine when she left here.

*Comment from Belfast shipyard
on the Titanic, 1912*

A pleasure shared is a pleasure halved.

Anon

Those who can do. Those who can do more, volunteer.

This was a tribute to the volunteer guides at Kew's Royal Botanic Gardens on their 20th anniversary

There is no such thing as waste: only stuff in the wrong place.

With thanks to architect Duncan Baker-Brown

Q: How long should a man's legs be?
A: Long enough to touch the ground.

J.D. Salinger, American writer

Sushi must have been created by two Jews thinking, 'How can we open a restaurant without a kitchen?'

Jackie Mason, American comedian

Wine is sunlight, held together by water.

Galileo

Madness is a relative state. Who can say
which of us is truly insane?

Woody Allen

Trust is a casualty of modern society.

Father Edward, a Benedictine monk

I am equal to anyone but superior to
no-one.

Shami Chakrabarti on BBC Radio 4

Physically I'm a chicken.
Mentally, I'm bold.

Jeff Bezos, founder of Amazon, on himself

Fear is a far more dominant force in
human behaviour than euphoria.

Alan Greenspan, interview by
Gillian Tett, FT 25.10.2013

I would be ashamed if I ever said anything
I didn't believe in, to get on personally.

Tony Benn, BBC radio interview

What's right is what's left if you do
everything else wrong.

Robin Willliams, America actor

A party full of 'likeable' people doesn't
bear contemplating.

Will Self

God help England if she had
no Scots to think for her.

George Bernard Shaw

As a coach, you are only a dancing bear
for the stars.

*Udo Lattek, with thanks to Just
Football's Robert Clucas-Tomlinson*

Anyone found here at night
will be found here in the morning.

Notice in Texas

There are few squeals so shrill as those
of society's winners defending their
advantages

Robert Shrimsley, FT 2.6.2016

The problem with the race to the bottom is that you might win.

Seth Godwin, Seth's Blog

She was famous for being the first person to be famous for being famous.

Wendy Holden on Tara Palmer-Tomkinson
who died aged 45 in February 2017

Last Word

The last word is from Donald Rumsfeld. He was US Secretary of Defense during the invasion of Iraq and his 'known, unknown' comment received wide publicity at the time. Here it is in full.

Reports that say that something hasn't happened are always interesting to me, because as we know, there are known knowns; there are things we know we know. We also know there are known unknowns; that is to say we know there are some things we do not know. But there are also unknown unknowns—the ones we don't know we don't know. And if one looks throughout the history of our country and other free countries, it is the latter category that tends to be the difficult ones.

Index

Editor's note: Most of those named in this book can be found in Wikipedia. The rest are mere mortals, including my friends and family.